LOVE**UN**restricted

Love Beyond the Boundaries of Safety

Book One

I0089624

LOVE**UN**restricted

Love Beyond the Boundaries of Safety

Book One

Author

Avis A. Mitchell

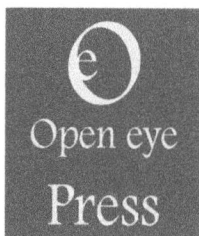

Published by Open eye Press

ISBN 13:
978-1-944662-31-8

Graphic Designer
MAS Graphic Arts, LLC

Original Drawing Designed by
Edward H. Mitchell

"LOVE" Artwork in the Background of the Photos was Created by
Lisa Marie Thalhammer

Printed in the United Stated of America

Preface

My thoughts on embracing and understanding my craft.
Meditating on how and what to share with the world.
I've tried to escape these feelings because it consumed all of me
It settled in my nature became what I breathed
My will was overtaken, I laid helplessly
stripped opened to my bear skin
Letting my truths be told, having me way too vulnerable
In each message, showing pieces
leaving me fully exposed
Trembling at the notion, releasing all control
Every word displayed, through my inner poet

Love Unrestricted, loves unrestricted!

Acknowledgments

This book is a testament of the many pieces of my life. Pieces that tell my truths, fill in my blanks, pieces that speak my souls peace.

An insight into the lives surrounding me and how my mind interprets the experiences of myself and others.

A dedication to my support for encouraging me, even when I wasn't sure of where I wanted this to take me, that constant push, drives me.

Thanks to my children, Edward & Amani for making me understand the meaning of life, love and beauty. They are my reasons for me to dream big, set goals and live life. If I want them to reach for the best within themselves, I need to show them how it's done. I have to show them that every dream deserves an opportunity to grow beyond imagination.

Thanks to my mother for being absolutely great. Life's lessons would have extended unendurable difficulties without the strength, without the confidence and without the fearlessness that she shows.

Thanks to Malik & Rashad for being phenonmeal brothers to me and outstanding uncles to my children. Showing my son how to conduct himself like a gentleman and emulating what my daughter should look for in a soul + mate.

So thankful for my Bestie, Aisha, for the loyalty, support and love that she continuously gives our friendship from an unconditional place in her heart.

I thank God every day for bringing these blessings into my life!

The Start of Something Great

Greetings Everyone!

Who Guides Me

My faith, hope and love comes from the breath of my mother. I've learned through my mother's unique, naturally giving, understanding, non-invasive, remarkable love. She has always exemplified the epitome of independence, making a way out of her way. She has shown incredible strength and perseverance through her life's journey and I'm blessed beyond words to have the opportunity to be an unconditional part of her world. Love Ya Moma

Eddie & Amani, the owners of my heart. They have the soul of my love, the pulse in my veins, touching my world more than words could ever articulate.

Who Was There

Love and appreciation to my little brothers, Malik & RaShad for always acting like my BIG brothers, so thanks for being exactly what a brother should be and thanks for marring two wonderful women I can now call my sisters (Kai & Earlisia). Special thanks to my entire family from Maryland, DC and Southern Virginia, without a loving family to love me, I would be ineffective. Cousin Cotton, love always from the sandbox. Thanks to the Queens; Aisha, Chanda, LaShone, Tiffany and Traci for forming this bond that we share and remaining my irreplaceable home away from home. And Tonio, making my different feel normal, my path walker.

Who Else

Arminta, LaTashia, Linda, Tammy, Kesha and the OSEC Ladies, thanks for the words of encouragement! Your support never goes unnoticed.

Who Touched Me

I've experienced my loves in the moments they were lived in and through them all, I have been given my stories. I cherish falling fast and hard in these unrestricted loves. Sharing myself in these times, I opened my heart to feel it all; the height of joy to the low of pain, and I loved every step. So as I wait for my "Perfect," I'm thankful to Love for keeping me, teaching me, for loving me.

But Why

Everyone in life has something that belongs to only them; something that can be done effortlessly by their hands; something inside of them dying to be released. I feel mine is the ability to make my situations flow by creating a chain of rhythmic words that pull you into my thoughts. My experiences and the experiences of others make for a good journey. Life has so many love opportunities; it shows the beauty in the beautiful and the ugly in the bad. All approaches to life are presented differently and received as such but it's that difference that makes life such a wonderful thing. Sometimes life requires us to observe from many angles in order to appreciate and understand.

Love screams softly; calming a storm or causing a rumble in the jungle. So be ready to Enjoy it, Learn from it, but most off all, Welcome it in. Listen and feel the many voices into life's greatest adventures of an Unrestricted LOVE.

Welcome to my stories into love.

Inspired by 'Love'
Dedicated to 'The Lost Ones'

Love...

the excitement rooted in your heart forever;

realizing you want the end more than the now;

a continually encore;

words spoken without being said, body movements when you lay down for bed, silent days and un-slept nights, miscommunication leading to fights, being held tight after a bad nights dream, living on one foundation;

not only feeling it when everything is good but at the times when your eyes are cried out, your head hurts and you have no more words to say;

knowing why all dumb things are done and why all foolish things are said;

the ability to make everything work; and

a creep, lurking in the cut, ready to pull you in.

makes me better!

A Journey Into My Continual Transition...

Our Love

Looking through a stained glass
we picture perfect
Smudged prints hide the deceit
in those moments of pain
Curved by the waves
our love is forced to compete
Covered by a blazing's fire warm smoke
the coldness settles in the dust
Visions of us spiral loose
grasping to pull together
to form what our love will be

The Effect

Your footprints imprinted by my bedside
where did you go
it's like you never existed
But cologne soaked sheets
and the linger of your smell
stains where you once claimed space
But the way you left me behind
to drown my nights in tears, damn shame
And after all I gave to your wants
without knowing how you would love me
I fell for the desire of more
your existences became my reason
I found love in your way out
In the seconds you gave
To an empty dream
made a lasting effect
on a cold reality

My Truth

If I was to sit waiting on you
to be that thing that awakens me
my days would pass in darkness
Living within this experience of us
has forced me to focus on who I am
and sometimes I don't like me
The part of me that is patience with you
The part of me that gives excuses
for the excuses you give to me
The part of me that puts up with the part of me
that puts up with you
Consumed in the idea
that who you are to me is enough
But as the people around me whisper
on the things I cannot see
Because I'm looking from the inside, out
I'm floating in my truth
that you do what I allow you to
and each day I give you tomorrow
to be the exact same person you were to me yesterday
Something must give
so I guess that will be me

Lost

Stumbled in my new path
with only my will
Strong enough to fail
thriving enough to scream help
Off centered in my balance
holding onto air
Determined to move still
and even in the light
I stand in the darkest shade
Carrying a heavy load of nothing
in a direction to everywhere
Midway emerged in total depth
I find myself out my lost

Let Go

Yesterday was our future
but as our future
slowly falls into a square circle
we don't seem to fit like before
Swallowed whole
you lost connection or did I let go
My wants separated your needs
or the need to want is gone
Feels like tomorrow will be our past
and our past ends the two of us
as we let go of today

The End

Time has convinced us
that we don't work
so let's walk away
before causing further hurt
Give us to someone else
end our loveless together
Erase the days and nights
crumble down bedroom walls
remove our body's scent
discard any signs that we were one
Travel different routes
to avoid chance meetings
Delete all points of contact
prevent ways of remembering
Forget these souls were once mates
and schedule our closing date

Let Him Go

To begin again
without my heart being captive
without my body craving him.
Effecting my mind, confusing my space
to end at a place where my wants no longer need.
I fight within myself to let go
relinquish this unhealthy obsession
Having his world collide into mines
but when he pulls me inside
to turn my insides, upside down
I lose the will,
and just like that his presence is gone
Left to start over
holding onto the beginning of my lost.

Alone

Feeling my way through
connecting with myself
as I flow through life to become.
No distractions altering my thoughts
reflecting on decisions
that hold tight to my path
Elevating my growth
to confidently move forth
Finding my purpose
with reasons to leave alone, alone

Motivation

What can be your motivation
to move you pass today
pass that steady pace going nowhere.
Is living in a shell that hard to break free,
so scared life will neglect you
that you stay locked within.
Nothing is definite but a try
Your willingness may work
but you will never know
if kept closed inside.
Remove those inhibitions
don't stand in contentment
Every time you doubt success
brings moments of failure,
Holding you in a space
a place to relucted to leave.
No progress, in no growth
nothing to believe.
So what can motivate you
to move you pass yourself?

Friends to Lovers

We became without even trying
feeling right together.
I want to grow in this life with you
creating a chance at forever
I want to learn every part
and lay all night in your arms
with each day pulling us closer,
without saying we belong.
And within our patience's
our hearts we have discovered
that we grew from being Friends
into becoming Lovers

That Feeling

Alone in my room
after days from your last touch
this feeling screams more
Night falls again
and I'm calling you over
to do what my body needs
You come in
as each breath gets heavy
your moves drown within
The walls close in
as you pull me tighter
Anytime, anywhere you can do anything

My Rock, My Strength

I found my rock
I found my strength
securely hidden away
underneath layers of guilt
buried in shame
with reasons that make no sense
scrambling through years of abuse
to uncover a bleeding heart
barely beating and severely bruised
looking for an escape
happiness dormant in a mix of confusion and lies
but with a will to push through
and overtake a weaken life
To lift the guilt
remove the shame
take back what was lost
throw the past away
unlock a new future
To my rock
To the strength I found in Me

Reality

Dreams of hope to become someone
buried in my darkest hours
Too scared to move forward
ideas are chaotic
the end begins my start
I scream internally
to shake from this deep sleep
I force my will
to lay my fears aside
Lose this insecurity
and face my reality

Energy

My energy is drained
from the many times
I had to carry you
in and out my life
My bruises ache
at this final heartbreak
So at this point
I'm no longer bothered
by not being bothered by you
Your lack of
has pushed my limits
I have nothing left to give
My emotions are tired
and this love moves aside
as the will in my heart
has used its last energy on you

My Goodbye

Is my presence a bother
Do you wish me harm
Now that we're over
And my existence is gone
You love someone new
So fast, so soon
Now I'm forced to move on
And gather myself
Discard all memories
Until there's nothing left
Take back my love
Reserve it for another
Let go of my pain
And accept that it's over
Cry a little longer
Then start my life fresh
Open up my world
To someone else

Reverse Roles

I don't want to love
I want to hurt some hearts
Lie to these brothers
with no remorse
Have his eyes crying out
losing his train of thought
While sitting home alone
catching migraines
wondering who I'm with
following me around
calling my friends
just to find out where I been
The thought of me cheating
makes him sick
I want to do some dirt
while he handles it
and with each complaint
I'll shift the blame
Reverse the roles
and play this man's game

In Love

Love is funny
how it changes from a maybe to a yes
Living each day in the seconds
to get a moment of what you put out
Wanting every action to assure a place of home

Life outside these walls
wonders how this stays so strong
Growing from the unknown into a future
on nothing but a promise of more

Heart beats louder
repeating its rhythm of affection
Feeding this undying emotion
unexplainable devotion

Causing senses to awaken
embracing it all
Showing how these two separate hearts
fell in love

Forever

My heart is pierced, by the loss of you
while my life races for closure
Decisions that left me mad and confused
my whole world flashed before me
Parts of tiny pieces that remained
words that hid the truth
Spoken by a familiar voice
the repeated lies you said
Abandoned hope
too tired to fight
in the battles I once engaged
My body cries
tears of hate
my soul's enraged
I surrender my control to deceit
believing in your truths
And as the pain crashes down
sometimes hard to bear
Forces me to swallow my suffering
as my heart gasp for air
This became my ending
what was to be never
Clinching to my last source
to breathe this last love forever

Rap:
It's a critical situation, my heart just stopped
Can't feel the beat, over the torn to pieces part
My brain doesn't rely the message,
that my heart is still alive
Divided in two halves, waiting to be revived
Holding still on the floor, my body goes cold
Panic sets in, as my senses go numb
Hurry to my side, to hear my love letter
Feel the loss of me, and breathe this last love forever

Heart. Beat

My plans were to erase the feelings of my heart beat
Battered and bruised due to the lack of
Constantly becoming the strength of two
When it's more than just me in this relationship
Traveling to foreign lands with friends
Forced to watch the sunset with no romance
Because there's no man here with me
And when I leave, should I just let it fall
Allow love to lose faith, with no fight at all
But he said my journey, should be traveled by two
And that he was to share my throne
Crowning me his queen
Because I deserve a roaring lion
to be the king of my jungle
Roaming pass my end
Where my borders come down
Loving beyond the boundaries of safety
Deep outside his comfort
To love on ever emotion
Being every part I need him to be
Rearranging his heart to beat with me

Thoughts of Destiny

My destiny travels to me
on a thin line of patience
collecting each thought at every stop
Waiting in this surrounding space
checking what works
what thing will last who should I TRUST
who should I let LOVE me

Learning Others Vulnerable Emotions
on a ride to transparency
Sharing our thoughts together
towards the meaning of you and me

The feelings I circle back to
all paths will cross eventually
Daydreaming of the moment
I catch up to my Destiny

Can This Be Love

Can this be love I'm seeing
Don't want to fall too hard
It's the perfect conversations
When I glance in your eyes

Can this be love I'm seeing
Missing you when you're gone
Not that attracted to you
But you're so handsomely fine

Can this be love I'm seeing
Not sure of what to think
So scared you may reject me
So I don't say a thing

Can this be love I'm seeing
In between the blinks in your eyes
Or is what I see just a reflection
Of the feelings I hold inside

Self Pain

She peeked inside
and noticed the reflection of her pain
caused by her words
by the uncaring way she gave
The feelings, internally engraved
destroyed by past hurt
impossible to live
struggling for self-worth
With hopes of growth and strength
the will to reject negativity
reject lies and disappointment
reject anger and abuse
Rejecting the her that lives in despair
but in this brokenness
failure holds strong
as she faces the fight to move on
With promises to get better
and not be that mistake
but as her world aches
she continues in self pain

On My Way

On my way there, I fell in love
But couldn't handle the feeling.
When opportunity came
to hide my thoughts
I grabbed it and ran with it.

On my way there, I fell in love
But didn't know it.
Now I understand what I didn't before
But there's no point to show it.

On my way there, I fell in love
But was scared to face it.
Stared it in the eye and turned away,
Now I'm paying for it.

On my way there, I fell in love
And now I'm longing for it.
Can't find it anywhere,
Had one chance and blew it.

On my way there, I fell apart
Took what you gave and crushed it.
Now I cry for ever doubting you
Cause on my way there, I lost you.

Part 1

Once you understand
That it wasn't me
Who asked you to call
You took it upon yourself
To speak to me at least five times a week

That it wasn't me
Who asked you for time
You took it upon yourself
To spend your free moments in my arms

That it wasn't me
Who asked you to assume
You took it upon yourself
To trust that I belonged to you

That it wasn't me
Who asked you to confide in me
You took it upon yourself
To tell me your feelings

That it wasn't me
Who asked you to believe
You took it upon yourself
To pray that my dreams became reality

Part 11

So now you understand
That it was you
Who I wanted to call
So I waited by the phone

That it was you
Who my days revolved around
So I was available

That it was you
Who blinded my eyes to other men
So I convince you that I was your lady

That it was you
Who I wanted to get to know
So I listened when you spoke

That it was you
Who I bared my soul to
So I fell in love

Thing Called Love

Fumbling through empty thoughts
In this thing called love
What qualities should he possess
Should he love me just as much

My heart is weak and fragile
Don't want it torn apart
Maybe this is why I'm so careful
When giving away my love

Although I'm longing to meet him
I'll leave it in the hands of faith
Am I deserving of my soul mate
Time and time I wait

Lost in thoughts of a true love
But all I see is despair
Why is this thing called love
When it should be called
it's not out there

Loss of Life

I live in my shadow
So I never get wet from the rain
The sun can burn at 100 degrees
And I never feel the heat

Wind that blows around me
Seems to fly right pass
The smile that glows when you're in love
Has never graced my face

I live in a world
that's so emotional
I live in this world
but only feel a Loss of Life

My Heart Can Back it Up

Due to your uncertainty
you question my love
No matter what you throw my way
my heart can back it up

These feelings for you are strong
and I can't stop the growth
Open up and feel my love
see deep inside my heart

Welcome what you avoid
understand it's not a game
Take all that you need
my heart will remain the same

I can make you happy
without a doubt
a pause or hesitation

I'm so certain in loving you
and it can only get better

My life needs you
with a promise of forever
This feeling is awaken
vulnerable to whatever
No matter what you throw my way
My heart can back it up

A Black Man's Body

Those sparkling brown eyes
I fall for every time
Those lips
that fit perfectly into mines
That smile
that melts me just like butter
Those arms
that hold me whenever
Those hands
that touch all the right places
That chest
I lay firmly against my face
The middle of your being
makes me warm inside
Giving me pleasure and creating a child
Those two strong legs
can stand alone
Carried by your feet
and the weight of your woman

Friends In the End

It was never complicated
Everything seemed to work
We never had to prove us
Our lives somehow merged
Never got tired of routine
We were lovers as well as friends
So now that it's over
And we have gone our separate ways
Can the pieces that completed us together
Break away as friends

The Loss

How do you cope with the loss of a love
When they were doing just fine
How do you convince yourself it's alright
When everyone around you cries
How do you tell their children
Without slowly breaking their hearts
That their mommy or daddy are gone
As the tears form in their eyes
Family members all around
Remembering each special day
Brothers Uncles Daddies
Even take a moment to pray
So how do you cope with the loss of a love
How do you say goodbye

The End Crept In

The end came so swiftly
I was not prepared at all
Nor was I ready to let go
I still feel what you somehow lost
What events led us here
I thought everything was intact
Undamaged, unbreakable
Left me completely relaxed
Fearless of nature's calling
Confident that death would be our ending
But what I couldn't see
I regret I wasn't fearing
Pretending this was infinite
When your intentions were to leave
No explanation could suffice
Nothing could rekindle this lost
I should have been more cautious
Instead of honestly believing in us

Not Ready

When the time is right
we can indulge in pleasure
Sharing our bodies willingly
openly loving each other
Laid in your arms
but dared not to kiss those lips
Laid with your body
as you whispered patience
Turned inside out
will the next time be right
Curious but reality cautious us
Scared of the consequences
Disease Pregnancy or AIDS
Never thought about it
the partners you may had
am I safe with you
are you safe with me
there's so much to lose
What if there's no protection
do we wait or follow through
Should we talk to our parents
family, doctor, friends
What would be our questions
I don't know what to ask
It's becoming so hard
because everyone is doing it
but I don't want to lose my life
over something I have no clue in
We hesitate more often
afraid to touch each other
The only thing we're sure of
is we're not ready to become lovers

Bye is Better

I know I brought this on myself
Believing he was ready after only a month
Stepped in and stepped up to a whole new game
Didn't give his self anytime to make this change
Came out of one and straight to another
instead of being friends,
we went straight to being lovers
Spending the night, practically moving in
Every waking moment was him and me
But he was the one to say it all
The "I love you's", the marriage,
the big house and cars
I followed his lead, being crazier to believe it all
I was so into him, didn't think I could fall
My commitment grew
I went so fast I couldn't stop
Couldn't tell him what I was really thinking,
just kept my mouth shut
And the timing was so off
I could sense it in his voice
But I was so scared of losing him,
I let nature take its course
He tried his best to make it work
but I knew it wasn't real
Obvious things showed me
This relationship should end
But I trusted his words, as he concealed the truth
He made all the rules and I played the fool
He was torn between being with me but loving her
The truth didn't seem real cause I knew the worst
I stared at reality to see what worked
Even though I loved him
I had to love me first

Two Years

I held her hand
Through that two-year transformation
Towards the end I let go
But she didn't even fight for me
Like she said she would
We both did a 360°
Now she lives in a better space
While my world is upside down
You don't owe me you
But why not try to
Because your heart skips a beat
without mines in it
I don't want to be adored
But rather have you madly in love
Let me be the one
You are willing to call your girl
She held my hand
Through those two years transformation
On October 8th she let go

Patience

How did I get to this point
Without you by my side
Why am I so certain
While you run and hide
I feel like a loose cannon
Can't smile or cry
Not sure if you loved me
Not sure of our last goodbye
You say you need space
While my heart just suffers
Internally I'll hurt
Until you get you together
I promise to be patience
And pray for your return
but once this heart heals
You can't have my love anymore

Two Hearts

What does it take
For two hearts to beat as one
Is there such a thing as falling in love
When the other has no idea of their wants
Will thoughts appear clear
Or will words speak fear
Can confusion be a reason to leave
Or is time strong enough to hold
What if opportunity slips by
Will the last chance be gone
Can emptiness search through the lost
Are there possibilities
That maybe one day
Two hearts can meet
That maybe one day
Two hearts can beat the same beat

Let Go

I love him so much
but he doesn't think so
He thinks I carried him
because I let him go
Letting go of someone
is the hardest to do
can't deal with the pain
my heart is going through
Can't let him see
that I'm needing him back
Stopped asking for his love
but it's his love I want
Distance drives me crazy
as I walked away
my heart was begging me to stay
Pleading for a second chance
to love on this pounding in my heart
The hold belonging to this man
I had to let go

The Motions

Why should I want my space
didn't I always want this honest kind of love
True, previous cats have influenced my thoughts,
have me thinking that my man is faking
but he cries to me, he smiles for me
he proves his love for me
even when I'm acting funny
he still hangs around
My fear pulls me back from giving my all
but he dismisses that and loves me hard
I want this doubt to end
before I lose his love

The Cheat

I thought he was the one
Until I found her number
Caught him calling her phone
Saw them cuddled during lunch
Constantly coming home late from work
With a smile on his face
Did I give too much of myself
Or just not enough
Everyday was a lie
a brutal reality
While I was in love with him
He was cheating on me

She

I left her,
as she promised to mend the pain
Tears fell slow,
on that sunny October day
I helped her grow,
while I lost my will
But my heart still loves,
through the hurt I feel
Hopelessness grew fast,
with each word she spoke
What I longed to hear
but couldn't trust any more
Assurance held no comfort
as the end became our beginning

Restart

Broken heart became crushed
need to rebuild my will to love
Mend the doubts
and handle the fears
Realized this disaster
changed my walk
Cleared my path from debris
put two steps forward
to restart my heart
Let go of the unwilling
allow the unseen
Open to the unknown
lose the hurt from before
With the past miles behind
I stand stronger
My heart I'm rebuilding
breaking down these walls
Shaped a new beginning
with every inch of my love

Past Meet Future

Your future can make you reopen
what probably took a while to close
Once you're over your past
why does your future bring it up?
If it doesn't affect us
why is it an issue
That's my baggage
I'm not asking you to carry it
Once it's discarded
that should be the end
My past is where it belongs
nowhere around here
I don't want to know yours
unless it's a need to know
just make sure your past
doesn't stumble forward
In future conversations
we will hear about each other
but in the content
that will not bother us
And our past shouldn't dictate
or stop our growth
but sadly it does
so face to face they stand
There's no telling the outcome
when the Past shakes Future's hand

Perfect

I saw perfect in my dreams
It trusted my love
From as much as I gave
To when it wasn't enough
It wanted my past
To see a future in it
Took time to listen
When I had nothing to say
Understood the journey
And what drew us here
Depended on the storms
To make things clear
Knew destiny was formed
By the steps that we walked
Perfect came through it
Without reservations
Welcomed in feelings
With no hesitation
Worked out our issues
Whenever they came
Perfect saw perfect
In every moment we made

Confusion

Yesterday was in my past
until tomorrow brought it up
Drunk on water
sober off this 5th of gin
No laughter behind this smile
my grin looks the silliest
Freezing in the month of June
dripping sweat in Christmas
Pressure builds
my soul burns open
My life needs a plan B
a way out this insanity
Too many things to do
I can't keep up with keeping up
My strength feels weaken
standing over my understanding
I question each move I make

Back In Your Bed

Uncovered years of buried feelings
deeply suppressed away from thought
Our last encounter was final
fatality left me dead, inside and out
Now I'm driving 15 miles away
to crawl back in your bed
rekindling the feelings
of last we shared
Memories repeat our nights before
how your touches sent me spiraling
Every part of you I craved
inviting the pleasure you gave
Every sexual moment
ran fire through my veins
Awaiting on the chance
to get back in your bed

Feeling Sound

Music speaks to my soul
through the rhythm it plays
echoing the beats of my heart
feeling the vibrations in the tone
waves create the passion
as the melody strokes
arousing sensations through the soft voice
the harmony stimulates the body
when the key note strikes the cords
rejuvenates desires
laying quietly in the tune
feeling how sound makes love

Our Meeting

I stare from a distance
at my secret weakness
Changed my path
with hopes to meet him
Have his attention of me
occupy his mind
Become his every need
control his every thought
Be a distraction in his life
become the desire he wants
Have our eyes to finally meet
and see I'm his missing part

My Love For You Grows

My time spent with you
just isn't enough
Need more hours in the day
with the one I want

I know you're learning me
want to see the good and the bad
I know to take it slow
but it's too late to turn back now

Can I say I love you
without scaring you away
Can I say I need you
and you feel the same
Can I say your heart
is destined to fall
Can I say my heart
is already yours

My love for you grows
in each moment we share

Doubt

When words are unspoken
feelings are unclear.
I told you I loved you
and you just stared.
Say what you're feeling
just speak your mind.
All our time together
and I can't tell what you want.
Am I seeing a bigger picture
that's just not there
or do you really feel it too
but too afraid to share.
Tell me your feelings
be honest and true.
I need to know
if this is worth going through.

Simple Love

I want to take us easy
falling for every piece
I don't want to move to fast
I want to feel every beat
Make this thing so special
that I bring a smile to your face
Feeling of love unlike no other
sharing this life together
You as my husband
and me as your wife

The silhouette at the beginning...

Past to Present

What's that something about you
that gets me caught in your smile
Your swag is so smooth
that charismatic style
I understand the hold
you have on your past
but it's my turn now
and I deserve my fair chance
So stop all the tears
the I miss you
the goodbye's
cause nothing you say
will break him down
His focus is here
and he's all mines now

My Side

I whispered a secret to my friend
didn't know if she could comprehend
the agony and pain I feel
within my skin.
The bad decisions that led me here
to this place of disappointment
situations that were not worth it.
Some words exchanged I can't take back
but the moments were heated
so my feelings spoke up.
The blame placed loosely
on these fictional facts.
Claiming victim but a willing participant
all dirt was brought to light
and although it hurt
the circumstances didn't change the circumstance
my in seemed harder to get out.
These feelings didn't grow overnight
they came from work and understanding
time and commitment
but the end brought less of that
and more of the bullshit.
Once upon a time, I woke to try
but in the end, our love just died.

Metaphorically Speaking

You're like a cup of tea
in the morning as I wake
Every formed cloud
that makes the raindrops
Unexpected sentiments
A hello or thank you
Music that expresses the soul
Grandma hugs and mommy kisses
Playing hide and seek with your first crush
Getting a license at 15 and 9 months
Baby girl falling to sleep in daddy's arms
An A average on a report card
Talking to an old friend for hours
Finding the right shirt for a date
You are, every emotion that feels great

Do You

When you're with someone else
Do you imagine me
Do you imagine my hair
That your fingers run through
My hips as you pull hers close to you
My legs wrapped around your waist
Your hands caressing my body
As you slowly kiss my face
Is it my eyes you see?
When you look at hers
Falling deep asleep and holding her tight
Do I consume your dreams
All through the night
Do you feel something missing
Deep in her arms
Do you imagine me
Do you

Loves Biggest Fan

Cheering from the rooftops
Yelling from the valley's low
A rocket to the moon to touch the stars
Just to bring one back to loves front door

In love more than yesterday
Today's already a sweet memory of my past
Can't wait to love again tomorrow
Forever Love will last

In for the passion
As well as the pain
Smile at the good times
Embrace everything
Love gives it completely
To everyone in its path
So open your heart
and become Loves Biggest Fan

Path to Destiny

Starting this journey
towards a greater expectation
A brighter present
Brings a glimpse into the future
The unknown can intimidate
but still the search is promising
Prepare my mind to welcome it
a future meant for me
With hope that dedication
is the strength I need
Trust that growth
can be something to depend on
Stand in perseverance
even through the hardest times
My will moves forward
towards the path to destiny

Unknown Destiny

So disconnected
don't recognize this feeling
so irritated in this life I'm living
Everything in my past
has opened my eyes
So surprising for me
I have no desire to cry
Don't know where to go
not in my right mind
Need some time alone
gather my thoughts somehow
Clear my mind
figure out where I belong
This constant emptiness
has taken its toll
Eating me alive
inside out
Opening to anew
however it comes
Time to live for me
instead of for everyone

Beautiful Feeling

What a beautiful feeling
completely unexpected
Like hearing an inner voice
whispering sweet nothings
So many similarities
I think this can work
Stuck in confusion
don't know how to explore
The scent is familiar
but this melts me more
The presence is dominating
which gives it that allure
Butterflies, sweaty palms deep
breath, long stares
I feel such a connection there
Tread lightly, hold fast
slow down, stay calm
want to rest in those arms
Where could this lead me
this beautiful feeling

Crushed Out

So out of the blue
my attraction for you
Not sure where it came from
or where it's headed
Never saw through these eyes
a person like you
And it's so premature to want you already
it's just something about you
that's driving me crazy
You consume my thoughts
feels a little scary
Not sure if you see me
or know what I want
but determined to tell you
so there is no doubt
I want your heart to hear mines
your mind to daydream me
our lips to finally meet
and you listen as I speak
Thoughts of how life would be
with you loving me

Ms. Carter

can't sleep, my mind is racing
she keeps entering my thoughts
crushed out, my desire now
but what does she want
to know her heart is taken
I'm careful with my words
don't want to overstep
and end up without her
so if I patiently wait
someday things will change
and the moment she starts to
give her heart to me

Unveil

For all it's worth
The door is now open
My mask has come off
The reveal is surprising
It's more than I thought
Lights are on, confusion is over
In the darkness no more
Cameras stopped flashing
The truth is now told
Unveiled my true secret
To those that I know…
Being honest with yourself
Makes it easy to be honest with everyone else!

She's Gone

At a loss for words
on an emotional rampage
the thought of never having her
due to things she can't tolerate.

I need to lose sight
shut these feelings down
disappear from wants existence
and just be a friend now.

That will suffice
if that's all that I am
accept the little she gives
without questioning

Become an open book
to build upon her trust
tell of my past encounters
with hopes she don't run

So I won't flirt again
or even make small jesters

I'll just look in her eyes
and be happy I met her

Finding Me, Loving Her

Tonight the tears poured down
can't understand this one,
my life again in someone else's arms.

My train of thought has no end,
day dreams, night dreams, fill my head.

Trying to shake this beautiful feeling
as hard as I can,
don't want to love her
at least not right now.

Need my time spent alone
by myself with just me,
sort through this change
and create the happiness I need.

But slowly she crept in
to no fault of her own,
but she's clearly unaware
I want to make her my home.

New Beginning

If I wanted to stop, it wouldn't
but they say it don't belong
If I try to change, I couldn't
cause it feels like home
I'm building my thoughts from what could be
even if it ends up not wanting me
It's still so beautiful
don't want the old way back
so I tiptoe through it
and welcome this new life

Thoughts of Her

Sit all night listening to her
learning what makes us work
To awake in her arms
kiss her morning lips
caress her face
and thank God she's here

Her sweet strong demeanor
has this hold on me
Teaching me her flow
opening to her world

Each moment is special
locked in my memories
Building a place
from the thoughts of her
showing how we can become one

Secure

All you give to this love,
is my secure
The energy you get
is the effort you put forth
The look you give a thousand times
I can't get enough of
All you give to this love,
I'm secure

Her Existence

The sun shines through passion's eyes
And arise from dawn's setting

The morning chill fills the air
When destiny starts speaking

The wind blows and flowers bloom
As beauty reveals her face

The birds sing and life exist
Once love begins her day.

As I Speak

I'm feeling comfortable in my skin
No more denying
To figure out who I am

Like a beautiful surprise
Knew it was something
Just couldn't figure it out

Day to day revelations
As each thought is formed
With eyes wide opened
In this life I'm reborn

Something so fulfilling
So perfect, so warm
So unaware
It was for me all along

Nothing temporary
Passion speaks the truth
Can't fight a substance
When it's calling you
All won't agree
But they must understand
These feelings I have
Are not going to change

Sincerely Virginity

Tell me how it came to be
me losing control of controlling me
Gave it to something that wasn't designed for me
Because we haven't met, he has not courted me
Hasn't sat around a table
to speak with the men that mean the most to me
How I allowed my own pressure
to peer pressure me
But did I need to learn the hard way
when I could have just listened
because my mamma walked my miles
just in different shoes
When now we don't speak, like we use to
When now I can't get back that special feeling
to present as a brand-new flavor never tasted
into my future life's consummation
It's now how I wish, that day played differently
Because I doubt I was ready to lie to my mother
have her drive me over for a 5:00 movie
that wasn't even showing
But my control had roamed off and left me stranded
So, I had to hitch that lost ride
even with the destination so clear
But a path is hard to follow
when your sneaking along in the dark
to a place you have no busy going
But still I ride
Even traveled to that place a little more than a few times
Before shit hit the fan and my business on blast
Once again control deserted me and left me opened to ridicule
Fussing and fighting, crying and contemplating
Is this the memory
I wanted this one time can't get back brand-new flavor never tasted
to be written in history for me
I think not but it is, none the less in stone
and no amount of deleting it can remove what was shown
So in that moment
I snatched back my worth and used what I knew
cause the next welcome pass will be in my control

Unforeseen Recovery

Your world is crushed out
You lost your whole to your half
Inflict hurt on deep scares
Become numb to the pain
Listen through the silence
To fight the worries away
Emerge from sadness
To reveal your strength
Cry that last tear drop
So life can start again
Wrap your arms around heartache
And let the healing begin

Unsaid

Unclear intentions
because our words were not shared
Miscommunication
because others interfered
The bricks came falling
before the foundation was formed
Stuck with the blue prints
with no chance to build up
The friendship is broken
your character destroyed
Forced to rebuild
lay the old plans aside
Nothing could save it
it was doomed from the start
Destruction came to us
and tore us apart
The mess that it made
left nothing but dust
All hope is lost
we gave up instead
Shattered our future
with things left unsaid

Illustrated Foreplay

The creation of your body,
was designed by my form
Warming my desires,
heating my world
Guide passionate strokes,
that fuel my soul's fire
Heighten senses,
caress my inner core
Shake beneath the structure,
functions move erratically
Internal sweats of panic,
beats pound over breaths breathed
Deeper sensations,
motions are faint
Incoherent movements,
as our bodies peak

Would You Still

Would you still love me
if I walked you to the deepest parts of my thoughts
Through the needs that I have
to the desires I want
To the passion that burns me
each pleasure unfolds
Through my inner feelings
dying to show
Hear these emotions
screaming out loud
Baring my soul
crying for more
Would you still love me
once I showed you my all

Anxiety

All that enters my mind
wonder how there's room for thoughts
The obvious becomes unclear
definite is questionable
Worried minds, troubled trouble
Holding on, gasping at wants
Need an exit to certainty
show doubt the way out
Take fear to the back door
release hesitation and breathe
Allow the path to lead me
Into my peace

Love Lost

Last night it rained on my soul
From the tears in my eyes
Forced to remove her presence
Completely erase her life
Show strength through my torture
While my love was ripped away
Broke down to my knees
This pain is hunting me
Feel the crazy in my thoughts
All sanity is dark
Crippled by nothing
Black outs cramp my heart
Alone with what's left
These flames burn slow
Flash back to warm stares
Now jagged as a knife
Internally I bleed
Because you have gone
Nothing more to hope for
Between me and love lost

My Morning

A late night special
need to be in your arms,
when the sun shines through want
to feel your soft lips
on the tip of mines

Alarm clock rings and the day begins
feel your hands pulling me back in bed

Inhale the scent of our morning smell
to lay in the warmth
of that evenings love making

Your tight embrace
with struggles to move
soft light strokes
that awaken my senses
as the sun rises
on a late night so perfect

Love Meets Misery

A broken heart
Opened and unguarded
Shattered into the pieces that laid
Losing loves beats
In the feeling of despair
Jaded and hurt
Struggling for closure
But nothing seems to work
Love becomes vulnerable
Anyone can have it
Pains continuous cycle
Becomes a harmful habit
Lessons never learned
Now history must repeat
Pressure built from worry thoughts
Lies formed its truth
Captive in a fear of hurt
Love meets misery

Rap:
Falling in love is easy
But a broken heart mends slows
Hurt plays on repeat
Rewinding its sweet hello
That laugh is gone, can't smile no more
Too weak and bruised, too battered and torn
Revisit the reasons, why it came this far
As I translate, the feelings we formed
I Iove you's, that use to roll from our tongue
Passion in caution, a burst of emotions
Feelings that blindly seen deception
its path crossed evasively
Dishearten misfortune
when Love Meets Misery

To Her isay

You deserve someone that heals the pain
and opens your heart to trust again
Someone that's secure enough in your love
to say no to your yes'
and yes to your no's

Have strong silent conversations
or one-word resolutions
An understanding of you
and the willingness to except
Chances to live and grow
from strangers to best friends

Your heart deserves it all
Every moment to
Learn Others Vulnerable Emotions
every moment to L.O.V.E. more

Reflection

In my reflection stands another me
One more different
Than what the world sees
With no end to the changes
Of my many faces seen

Strength in knowing
Of what has happened last
Weakness in tomorrow
Of those things yet come to pass

Giving me in the moment
At the time it is needed
Is not true forever
As things turns anew

Scattering around in uncertainty
Brings life full circle
To where my world resides
Back to the understanding
Of my many reflections inside

Together We Love

You got here
through the dreams in my eyes
by the strength of my love
from the time that I gave

I got here
through your reasoning
by connecting to your thoughts
from the overlap of our world

Now together we love

Past Tense

In those moments with you
I loved plentiful
Enough so much I loved for you two

In those memories I can recall
You giving your all
More than one person could ask for

In those times of you and me
It was for you and I
Building something that we shared
Feelings for the both of us to remember

The Struggle

As tears form in my eyes
I stop the need to cry
I will be stronger than my struggle.
After confusion sets on chaos
My will to fight is weaken
But I struggle through this battle for some sort of peace
Some overstanding of this mess
Because my understanding just can't be
The sense of where my path is leading me.
I thought it was those I was choosing
But as I look deeper in
It's the lack in me that repeats
This compromising me
Willing to sacrifice my wants for others needs
With constant reason after reason and excuse after excuse
I sell my soul for someone else's satisfaction
Undemanding of my own
I allow a way for unvalued years
I think the little you gave is enough.
But I'm greedy with love, submissive to love
If you cannot give it, please don't speak it
Because I rather not see you squirm from it
And as time proves unsure love gives excuses why it cannot
I will not be accepting them
These excuses ache my back
My stomach, legs, hands and feet cramp from reasons you cannot.
In these moments, my struggle could not hold, my life would need more.
After years of you being satisfied with me giving
Try overcompensating your feelings
Because in the end I'm a hopeless romantic
That sips until the last drop
And you still can't conceive that thought
My love is in everyone I touch
So rather I'm with her or he's with me
It will come dressed fully
With no reason to make excuses
With no struggle to fall in love.

Love Gone Bye

Is your love big enough
to search for me when I'm gone
Will your heart ache
til' I'm found
Does panic block your blood
and burst through your veins
Do you unravel
because I was the glue to your everything

Has emptiness caused you to cry
have you screaming from the pain
Creating an ending of forgetfulness
so thoughts don't include me
and memories are erased
forcing the love you felt
to spiral away

Destroyed

Pain is the hurt I feel
But my heart doesn't understand
Can't figure it out

My love should have been cherished
Instead she was careless
Ripped to shreds
In the blink of an eye
No remorse, no regret
The power she had
Changed my life

Peeled away layers of trust
Dressed in deceit and lies
My eyes cry out
I gave her a heart of love
And she returned it in stone
Torn to pieces
Without a second thought

Disgraced and humiliated
The more I gave
The harder the hurt

Want to distance that life
This emptiness is on me
I blame this lost on love
All of who I was
She destroyed

My Past

So tired of not knowing
Feels like this life is not mines
Don't know what I'm holding
Because our time is over

But still my steps show caution
Living in past tense
As my future looks back

See pass my past
Move me away from this darkness
But time moves in rewind
So tired of trying
Owned by what was left

After the last goodbye
My thoughts become heavy
To everything unknown
My past fooled me
Left me lost

But only prayer can move me
Through my turmoil
Clear my way clean
To bring peace to my home

Another Night

Grabbed my bags
for an overnight stay.
A shoulder to cry on
to wash out my pain.
Don't want to feel
the right in this wrong
just want this throbbing headache gone.

My life is on replay
as the pressure builds up.
Knees go weak
My pain begins to hurt.

Closed the bathroom door
to gather my tears.
Love songs play loud
and rings in my ears.

Catch my break down
before I fall.
Slept away my pain
and start fresh tomorrow.

Let Me Go

I heard enough of the lies
the thought makes me cry

Release your keep on me
and consent to this kiss goodbye

So many years captive to your hold
Make room in my life for another love

Introduce me to a world without you in it
Show me that emptiness fades
and there's more to offer
than the nothing you gave

Help me move forward, from this pain
Admit that you can't be, forever to me

Our Beginning

Does the darkness cling to the stars
As the universe offers peace in the night

Can the speed of light
Erase years of life
While the atmosphere burns a barrier to the core
Depths beneath the sight of survival

The elements of color
Reflect from absorbed energy
Aiding in the escape to the horizon's surface

Flutter around in endless time of lost
Synced to comets obscure paths

A flare rejuvenates intervals in travel
The field of view filters evolution
Gravitating to undeclared structures
Impacting the start of our beginning

Who I Am

As I awaken to a dream in hand
With many years of thoughts written down
Visions and ideas of how the world would see
A plan of sharing these stories through me
An insight into my passion
Similar experiences to everyone else
Long awaited by family and friends
Welcome to the journey of Who I Am
I am who I am
Defined by so much
Guilty by association
Of who I let in and whom I kick out
I'm a mess, a handful but I'm as sweet as pie
I'm a piece of work, a piece of everyone you meet
My mind has alter egos
Jumping in and out of personalities
I am a creator of two
My nerve wreckers, breath takers,
my continuous love
I'm my own heartbeat
I don't base my love on what you give
But rather how you portray yourself
I can date for 2 years as a friend and fall in love
Or go 7 years strong and still end up alone
I still would have given my all
Because my love is me
And you're sure to feel something
If you stay here long
So don't fight or resist it because love is who I am
I am my creation
The thoughts are made when the ink is laid
Memories of the past experiencing my now
Reminiscing to share with my future self
I get so excited when I see

Who I Am

con't

What my mind comes up with
Sometimes there's no thought until I write
And it ends up being called the unknown
I like creating things that make you think
New meanings each time you read
And it's so sweet when I can hear a beat
And write from the rhythms in the melody
Or listen to a friend
and speak their secrets through me
So don't sue me if your life is mirrored
At least you know I was listening
So as I sit down to sheets of paper,
the dictionary and my playlist tuned to
SiR, Syd, Caroline Smith, Jhene and Alina,
Sabrina, Lianne La Havas, and 6black
I write until my fingers bleed
Because I press so hard on the page
As if my ideas would leave
That's just the passion behind me
So as you awake to read the poetic lines
With each page turned, I welcome you in
To the re-introduction of Who I Am

A Letter to Perfect

I don't mind telling you that I have fallen in love.
I have fallen in love with your conversation
with your sweet smile, with your long stares
with your gentleness, with your openness,
I have fallen for everything that is you.
The special way you put things
always give me comfort and assurance.
You've become such a dependable loyal friend.
Our bond is built on the time we've shared
and the trust that has grown from it.
I've never felt so comfortably close as I do with you,
I realize this is what I've been wanting.
I want my search for perfect to stop in your arms
because before you…
I never know what I needed in my life,
until you let me into yours.

Space for your thoughts...

Read between love lines...

love by your means

love again and again

love all emotions

love the submissive in the dominant,
the dominant in the submissive

love the surprises

love differently

LOVEUNrestricted

Me...

If I was to think about how I would introduce myself from one central thought, I think expressing myself within the confinement of that thought would suggest me as a raving lunatic. I believe I absorb a piece of everyone I encounter, so I can't very well explain my evolution of self when I'm so intertwined with the many constant growing differences of the world. Like a lot of us, I present myself to others in the manner that is necessary at the time. Still interacting as myself, I just present the part of me that is best suited for the situation. So with that understanding, I introduce myself as an assortment of flavors, an oxymoron, empathic, neurotic, conscientious, finicky, introvert, optimistic, compulsive, unsuspecting type of creation. I'm a bit of everything, just ask my alter egos whom seems to handle me very well.

@arry.day_life

arry.day <u>of my</u> life
gives me incredible journeys to share
gives me better understanding of my choices
gives me a clearer perspective of life
gives me the will to grow creatively
gives me the opportunity to challenge the day before

Peace Blessings & Eternal Love

My Artist. My Son.
My UNrestricted Heartbeat

My Muse. My Daughter.
My UNrestricted Heartbeat